riverton
AND BEYOND

A COLLECTION OF DRAWINGS & STORIES BY JOHN HUSBAND

Foreword

On the 28th of March 1996 I published my first drawing for the recently resurrected "Western Star" newspaper.... Bill Moss, a longtime friend and retired photo-engraver, bought a property out in Riverton soon after I did and, as expected, we found that the historic town and surrounding district was a very special place and that a community newspaper was a must. The "Western Star" was first published on the 15th of November 1873 ... in the late 1880s it was published by the proprietors Galloway and Burns on Wednesday and Saturday. The first newspaper was the "Riverton Times". It was established in about 1864 but it only lasted a short while. The "Western Star" finally ceased its operations in 1947 after 74 years.

I've been drawing and writing about Southland for more than 35 years and a lot of my more favoured locations have been in the western district and in particular the Riverton region. I've found an endless range of subjects and if I was confined to one area for the rest of my working life I wouldn't repeat myself very often. Luckily there are still a number of classic "turn of the century" residences to record and of course the charm of the harbour with its variety of fishing craft and quaint jetties and wharf. Another of my favourite areas is the magnificent estuary — its many moods a constant source of enjoyment for an artist. Riverton is enjoying a well deserved revival with the recent addition of two fine café bars, gift shop and a variety of hotels — not as many as there were in the early days (15 at the turn of the century) but certainly enough to suit the tastes of most people.

For those expatriate Rivertonians, I hope this book brings back a few memories. For the locals, I hope I've portrayed our wonderful district as you would want.

John Husband

Index

Published by John Husband
34 Marne Street, Riverton

© 1999 John Husband

ISBN 0-473-06483-9

Printed by Craig Printing Co. Ltd,
67 Tay Street, Invercargill,
New Zealand.
Email print@craigprint.co.nz
Website www.craigprint.co.nz

First Impression 1999 – 144875
Second Impression 2000 – 147336
Third Impression 2001 – 153323

55 Riverton Road

When I drew this stately villa at 55 Riverton Road, it was being repaired and restored so I can be excused for showing a gap in the verandah decoration. I hope the present owners will forgive me!

The early Bay Villa or T. House shows a combination of the cottage style and the simple villas of the 1890s. Decorations on the gables, on the barges and under the verandahs were a feature of these gracious wooden homes . . . These homes began to appear around 1895. They were at their peak in 1910 and were still being built as late as 1915. This design was followed by the first of the wooden bungalow . . . Around the district there are many examples of this design and considering how much timber was milled in the province it's not surprising that there were relatively few brick or concrete homes built in the early days of Riverton's settlement . . . It's hard to imagine a villa as beautiful as this being built in any other material but wood. This home is well balanced and on a slightly elevated section which gives it a very commanding appearance.

This is one of Riverton's architectural treasures . . . Let's hope more of them have life breathed back into their frames so we can enjoy our history for many years to come.

Riverton Wharf

Scenes like this are what Riverton is all about for me. Fishing boats like these lying quietly at anchor waiting for a change in the weather so they can get out into the strait or Fiordland or anywhere else round our picturesque south coast. I don't even care too much if there are no boats tied up at these old moorings . . . I just love the planked walkways that lead to the wharves. The handrails have buckled in the sun and the piles appear to have shifted giving the walkway the appearance of a quietly meandering garden path . . . in all the time I've lived here I can never remember seeing anyone repairing these marine sculptures — perhaps the sea spirits do it at night . . . who knows!

John Husband...'95

OREPUKI COURTHOUSE

8

Orepuki Courthouse

Orepuki now stands on its third site, originally it stood at Monkey Island a little to the south of this now quiet village. In those days (the early 1860s), many hundreds of prospectors were busily engaged extracting fine gold from the beach. As the prospectors moved inland so did the township to the Garfield site. In 1885 the railway arrived and the township moved yet again to its present site. At the turn of the century there was a population of more than 3,000, thus justifying the building of this once elegant wooden courthouse. No doubt many a "Hard Case" miner stood, head bowed in the dock in the busy days of the mining of gold, coal, shale, iron and platinum. In 1879 the N.Z. Coal and Oil Company was formed in London with a capital of £180,000 ($440,000). Most of this capital was poured into Orepuki and a gigantic shale works was erected. So pungent were the fumes of sulphur they tarnished even the coins in the miners pockets. The works closed abruptly, amid many rumours, in 1902 and since that time the population has gradually declined. Now it is a quiet centre for the farming community. Sadly the wooden Courthouse has been demolished and so we lose another link with the past.

Cosy Nook

I've drawn and written about this little gem many times, so many in fact that I've lost count. I was driving home from work the other afternoon and the weather was perfect — perfect for an artist anyway! We'd just experienced our first frost for the year, during the previous evening, and we were left with one of those astoundingly clear crisp days when everything was shown in the sharpest relief — the paddocks were so green and the sky so blue that it's difficult to describe . . . However I drove on over the bridge turned right and headed towards Colac and the wonderful coastline beyond . . . I was looking for a belt of windblown Macrocarpas that I'd spied a month or so before around the Mullet Bay area . . . I found what I came for, did a sketch and carried on just to have another look at this "Cornwall Coast" lookalike! Even though the weather was fine and calm the sea was pounding those unique rocks to a foam, but once again it held my interest till the sun dipped down behind the hill that shelters the Bay . . . I drove home after a day's work very satisfied indeed. If you haven't been to Cosy Nook for a while, go on a blustery winter's day —- it's a treat!

Bowing to the Wind

I wander often along Highway 99 between Tuatapere and Colac Bay, dodging into Wakapatu, Monkey Island, Round Hill, Ruahine and Lake George and every so often a cluster of these tortured Macrocarpas presents itself . . .

It shows the huge strength of our ceaseless prevailing wind, but it also shows us how resolute these hardy trees are, being able to survive 70 or 80 years of salt laden force . . .

How did they survive the first few years? I'm sure the farmer didn't coddle them with wind cloth as is the case today. But what fascinates me are the shapes the trunks and branches have assumed over the long years . . .

I'm sure that if a sculptor had set out to create something like this he would not have succeeded as nature has. I've heard more than one person make derisive remarks about these tortured trees saying "Who needs to go to Puysegur Point when you can experience winds like this?". I find some beauty in every one of them.

Lodge Aparima

In 1883 Lodge Aparima 1617 met on the Tuesday after each full moon — why I do not know... only a member of the Brotherhood would know this... On consulting my collection of early business directors I found an entry which told me that in 1891 the worshipful master was one J. Paterson and his acting secretary was Mr. John Petchell... His family and possibly himself were also involved in the early Church of England in Riverton. There were at least two other friendly societies, The Wallace Lodge of the Independent Order of Oddfellows and The Sons of David Lodge of which Mr. J. Paterson was the secretary... wasn't he a busy fellow! Another member of the Paterson family, Helen, was head teacher at the Wild Bush School from 1893 till 1896. This building was finished in June 1910. Where the Lodge met before this time I couldn't establish but no doubt someone will know. I've drawn dozens of Lodge buildings throughout New Zealand, all of them vaguely similar but each one having its own characteristic touches. Some are brick, some are concrete like this and others are built of local material like the stone temple in Arrowtown.

Kohi Kohi's Cottage

"After extensive negotiations with the Ngatimamoe chiefs of the locality, Captain John Howell ascertained that by marrying a Maori woman of noble blood he would not only become a person of great influence in the tribe but would also be the recipient of large grants of land. Eventually an alliance was arranged for him with a young Chieftainess named Kohi Kohi Patu who lived on Centre Island . . . The marriage ceremony was a most picturesque affair and was attended by all the Maoris and white people of consequence in Murihiku. Immediately after the ceremony he took this magnificent specimen of Maori womanhood to Sydney for the honeymoon." So wrote J. C. Thomson in a collection of stories of early Riverton he compiled prior to his death in 1934. Eva Wilson wrote in 1975 that on the return journey after the honeymoon in Australia, John Howell brought with him a load of gum timber to Riverton with which he built his bride a sturdy cottage. Two bedrooms, a parlour, and a kitchen. It was roofed with wooden shingles and has a verandah across the front — a fitting home for a chief and chieftainess. It was built around 1837 or '38 before the birth of their son George and still stands today stubborn and sturdy on the area known as the Kaika and proud to be at least 158 years old!

It's indeed pleasing to see that this historic gem has been well maintained and if you are of a mind to look at a piece of real Riverton history you'll find it over the road from the school in Princess Street.

A Resting Place with a View

If you're spiritually inclined you may have given some thought as to where you will lie after death . . . your final resting place . . . ! The historical Riverton cemetery is indeed a resting place with a view — a view of river, estuary and whitebait stands. I can just imagine some of my few whitebaiting acquaintances booking a spot now with their feet pointing towards their little rickety stand! Whenever I go to a new area and want a bit of background I first go and talk to the locals in the pub, then off to the local cemetery and in a very short time you've got a potted history of the place. . . very simple and accessible. One of the noticeable features of very old gravestones is the sad recording of the deaths of young children and teenagers . . . in the late 1800s and early 1900s life expectancy was very short as is evidenced by the inscription on this headstone — it is the last resting place of Catherine (Kitty) Degan, daughter of Edward and Catherine. She died on the 14th March 1906 aged 17 years, but the greatest sadness was that their infant sons, James and Jeremiah lie with their sister. As is still the practice the makers of this fine white marble monument is inscribed at the base. It tells us that Kingsland and Ferguson were responsible and I wonder if monumental masons ever wander among the headstones admiring their handiwork?

A Well Weathered Barn

I've been driving past this piece of history almost every day for the last six years and it was only recently that I decided to get it down on paper, just in case the unthinkable happened . . . Grocer Brinsdon owns it now but at the turn of the century it was farmed by Jack McNaughton's grandfather John. The land was leased and the property ran from the hospital to the Otaitai Bush road. This view of the barn faces east and Jack McNaughton told me that he replaced the original weatherboards many years ago but considering it was built between 1900 and 1904 the beech 4x2 framing and the wooden piles have withstood the ravages of time and weather very well. It's a classic Southland barn design and out of sight in this drawing there was a feed loft. Jack tells me that when he was a child the bags of feed were thrown up into the loft with brute strength.

These days Ian keeps his collection of birds of all descriptions cosy and warm in this slice of Riverton history.

Long may it defy time and weather and last another 50 years.

Church of England

In 1858 Bishop Selwyn paid one of his visits to Riverton, among those christened in that occasion was Mrs H. S. Pankhurst. Two years later on 1st May 1860 a meeting of the Church of England members was held with the object of erecting a church. On the 3rd of February 1862 tenders for the erection of the church were dealt with. Galliot and Thystrup £130 ($260) Belbin and Small £175 ($350) and Flack and King £217 ($434). It was resolved to accept the lowest tender, subject to certain additions to be made to the specifications.

The first resident clergyman was the Rev. W. F. Oldham. In 1869 a Bazaar was held to raise funds and as a result the funds were used to complete the building of the church tower and to shingle the south side of the roof with "Hobart Town" Shingles. At a meeting in 1869 it was proposed by Mr Surman and seconded by Mr Instone that the church be called and known as St. Mary's.

The last service in the old church was held on the 5th of January 1902 and on the following Sunday (the 12th) this new church was dedicated under the title of St. Mary the Virgin, by the Bishop of Dunedin the Right Reverend S. T. Neville. In 1905 it was decided to build a Vicarage. In 1937 the Mills Family were known to have served the church and attended services regularly for 75 years. I wonder if there are any members still attending?

John Husband...

'RAILWAY BRIDGE, RIVERTON'

A Cause For Concern

In recent times the Southland Regional Council received an application for a resource consent from the Department of Survey and Land Information to remove a structure in Riverton and this started a lot of discussion in the town!

The structure, of course, is the Railway Bridge over the Aparima River Estuary. A landmark I've enjoyed drawing for many years. This view is of the trestle bridge on the South End of this remarkable structure which is in fact three very difference structures . . . Starting from just beneath the Aparima Tavern we have the familiar home-type timber truss frame, then the Stone Causeway which links the trestle and plank structure in the foreground. I can't think of another such railway bridge in New Zealand and it seems a shame that it took the authorities and the locals so long to start talking about its future. The building of the link with Western Southland was begun in 1902 and officially opened (no doubt with a flourish) in 1905 . . . Try and imagine the back breaking work that went into carting the stone (probably by wheelbarrow) to construct the causeway. Looking at it today, one must admire the brute strength, brawn and brilliant craftsmanship of these pioneer builders of our rail system.

Dr. Trotter's Home

I did the drawing of the Trotter house nearly 20 years ago before the present owners began restoring it. Then, the giant Monkey Puzzle tree stood commandingly in the front garden which was overgrown. If you looked very carefully into the long grass you could trace the concrete curbs and paths that defined a once fine gentleman's garden. Dr. Trotter was born in Invercargill in 1866, attended Woodlands school and Nelson College before going on to Otago University to study medicine. He completed his studies in Great Britain, graduating a Master of Surgery and for several years practised in London Hospitals. On returning to New Zealand he settled in Tapanui with his bride Elizabeth who he had married in London in 1890. His next appointment was as superintendent of the Wallace and Fiord Hospital in Riverton which lasted 34 years. He was a Borough Councillor for several years before becoming Mayor for 20 years. This long service was rewarded by the presentation of an illuminated address by residents in 1944. Part of which proclaimed "for as much as through half a century you have ministered to ourselves and to our children in our times of sickness and have healed our hurts and comforted our spirits and between times you have presided over our councils and granted us benefit of your knowledge and wisdom for these many kindnesses our hearts and thanks go out to you and we present this token of our grateful thanks and affection, hoping that you may long be spared to dwell and prosper in our midst . . . signed by the Mayor A. E. Philp." Such was the strong feeling and affection for this fine citizen, Dr. N. G. Trotter. He died aged 88.

Bill Moss's Place

. . . well it's not where he lives but it is where his "chooks" live, and it's typical of many farm buildings in Southland. Most of them start out doing one job and finish up doing another! I don't know if the previous owner built this as a hen house but it certainly does the job for Bill's birds . . . Bill used to be my neighbour when we lived in the city and many's the time we put the world to rights over the back fence. I told him one day that I'd bought a property in Riverton and not long after he announced he'd done the same and here we are, years later, with the best lifestyle you could imagine . . . A while ago he discussed with me the possibility of bringing back to life the town's original newspaper. For those of you who don't know, Bill (in a previous life) was a photo engraver and he was able to bring many years of printing experience to this new venture. I'm sure you'll agree that it's been a wonderful success. I've been wanting to write a piece about this fellow for some time now and share with you his interests and the work he's done for the community, like the senior citizen's hall and of course local body affairs — this will probably embarrass the hell out of him but I'm willing to take the consequences. You the reader must know of many other locals who deserve a few thanks for what they do for the community — let me hear about them . . .

The Rocks Post Office

This is not on old building by Riverton standards — it could have been built around 1937, which was the year the town celebrated its first 100 years. Then why did I draw it in the late sixties? Well I was told that it was the Post Office that served "The Rocks" area and I haven't found anyone who has disputed it . . . I wondered at the time, during what years it had served this purpose, but assumed that as there were Post Offices in places like Parawa, Garston, Colac Bay and Hirstfield then surely "The Rocks" deserved one! For the record, in 1891 Riverton's Postmaster was Mr W. Hutchinson and out at Colac Mr H. Nickless was the Post and Telegraph boss . . . How times have changed! Can you remember when Thornbury had a very large (for the country) Post and Telegraph office, but you must cast your mind back to remember just what the Post Office did in those days. Telegrams, telephones, money orders, motor registration, pensions and a savings bank, to mention just a few services. But the thing I remember most about the village Post Office was that it was the focal point — A Meeting Place.

The Corner Drapery — Orepuki

Orepuki has always held a great fascination for me, mainly because I first saw it in the late 50s when it was a bustling little township complete with hall and picture theatre. Neil McAlister had the garage and David McNay's parents had one of the grocery stores. Phyliss Popham had the other shop which seemed to be open all hours. Bernie Thomas and Alf Mason were the butchers and the shop in the foreground was founded in 1893 by the Adamsons . . . McDonalds had this shop when I first visited "Jim Fish the Baker" and in this same block his wife Betty held court in a shop which sold groceries and of course their fine bread and cakes. The only alteration which seems to have been made to the buildings in this street since they were built in the 1890s is the relatively new verandah on the corner shop. Unlike the shops in later years, the villages always had a row of very individual business premises — similar in design but so different in character. Otautau, Tuatapere, Riverton and Riversdale have managed to remain pretty much the same with their single main street, wooden and brick facades and those wonderful verandahs all at different heights! Now here's a bit of sheer trivia! In the 50s there lived in Orepuki four families by the name of Fish, Bone, Finn and Herron . . . Coincidence? I think so . . .

The Boat Shed

Driving home over the bridge each day for nigh on seven years, I've looked at an old boat shed, complete with dinghy, standing amidst rocks and flanked by a tiny white sand beach . . . I've said to myself almost as many times as I've crossed, "I just must go down and have a closer look at the shed, the rocks and the stone retaining wall that runs off the end of the bridge" . . . Well not long ago I finally got round to doing that very thing and after a very pleasant walk I sat in the sun and made this drawing.

I learned one thing from this little excursion and that was that someone still uses the shed and the dinghy because on the day I was there the tiny craft was away on an adventure and the following day I noticed it had returned to its safe haven . . .

Go and have a look one day — the stone wall is well worth looking at.

The Daniels' Home

Theophilus Alfred James Daniel was the ninth child of Thomas Daniel and his wife Anna Maria. He was born on the 30 June 1817 at the Anchor Inn, in Hastings, England which his parents owned, as did their parents before them. The Anchor Inn is still in use after all this time . . . We here in New Zealand would have pulled it down and rebuilt it many times — the English have a different attitude towards their history haven't they! However this young Theophilus went to sea at the age of 17 as a midshipman on board the "Hercules" a ship commanded by his oldest brother Captain Thomas Brown Daniel. The "Hercules" brought the first free settlers to Australia and fate stepped in when the ship was almost wrecked on Farewell Spit in Cook Strait, finally making land in Port Nicholson. Theophilus met Captain Howell in the port — went south, met and married Elizabeth Stevens and eventually built this fine wooden house at 85 Palmerston Street. I drew this portion of the house before the present restoration began because it was the only house of its type, in this very historical town of Riverton, that represented a true colonial design and thanks to family descendants it has survived and the restoration seems to be progressing well. Theophilus Daniel was a Justice of the Peace, a member of the Provincial Council, an M.P. for Wallace and the first Mayor of Riverton. He entertained extensively and one of his more famed guests was Governor George Grey . . . Next time you pass the house reflect on the history of this very important dwelling.

The Water Tank — Orepuki

The small unhurried village of Orepuki on the south east end of Te Wae Wae Bay is but a shadow of its former self when it hosted more than 3,000 people at the turn of the century . . . Orepuki translates to "Crumbling Cliffs" . . . The name is a corruption of the original Aropaki which means "Bright Expanse" — the scene the Maori party witnessed as they emerged from the dark dense bush, and looked upon a sparkling bay. They most certainly wouldn't have looked upon a railway water tank as railway didn't come to this part of Southland until the 1880s. When I arrived in Southland, Orepuki had a typical country station complete with all the trappings including a beautifully crafted tank on a stand. I found among my references architectural plans of a tank which told me that it sat on 30 inch concrete pads set 18 inches into the ground. The floor and staves were kauri or totara (if available). The stand timbers were of Australian hardwood and the dowels in the kauri floor planks were jarra. Quite a formidable structure by today's standards and think of the fine work done by the coopers. The last time I travelled through Orepuki I spied this same tank lying in a paddock by the highway . . . Wouldn't it be great to see it re-assembled in the railway reserve as a visual monument to pioneer railway in Southland.

D.PHILL
M13717

Whitebaiter's Refuge

This structure looks like it started life as a caravan. It's gone now, but when I drew it more than ten years ago it was in reasonable shape, compared to some of the shelters. The name crudely painted on the wall is D. P. Hill and the Registration No. is M 3712, whatever that means! No doubt it will jog someone's memory. In the background is the headland on which is perched our very historic cemetery beneath which the Aparima River wanders down towards the Jacob River Estuary. I took a wander around the "Whitebait Village" the other day and found that since last season quite a number of the stands and cottages had been "tarted up" — some of which looked positively smart. This year the bait are running in greater numbers than I can ever remember, no doubt making the long, sometimes chilly vigil well worth while. At high tide this stretch of water is a beautiful sight but maybe I'm biased . . . I've painted and drawn the estuary from every vantage point and every day it looks different.

Towack Street Villa

What an absolutely stunning view from the verandah of this Grand Old Lady of Riverton!

The design was known as "The Bay Villa". I believe it was built in the 1920s by local builder W. R. Pankhurst. The style was first seen in about 1890 and was continued on until the twenties. Another name given to this house was the "T. House" on account of the shape assumed by the floor plan. Decorations on the gable, on the barges and under the verandah became the order of the day. The verandah had the characteristic bull-nosed roof and the fretwork under the verandah was either cast iron or, in the case of this Towack Street home, wooden.

The gables gave space for imagination! In the case of this house the finial is missing from the top of the gable but where it originally carried on down the face can be seen in the shape of those gently curved battens — altogether a very pleasing design.

Another feature of these fine villas are the wonderfully crafted chimneys. The chimneys on this house are about average for the times but certainly surpass those of the present day. I suppose it's only a matter of time before brand new homes of this design will be appearing. They will be expensive but — oh so elegant!

Thornbury Junction

In 1892 R. Foster was not only the host of the Junction Hotel at Thornbury but also was a merchant with Whittingham Bros. and Instone and ran the Railway Refreshment rooms — busy fellow! But wait there's more! He was also listed as the local storekeeper. This is according to the Mills and Dick Directory of 1891. The stationmaster was a Mr T. F. Roskruge and blacksmith A. Weir was also the local wheelwright. Mr Gilchrist was the schoolmaster and the bootmaker was B. Hancock.

Licensees through the years have included Rob and Paula Dixon and names such as Turner, Drake, Hannah, Tisdale, Williams and Wybrow are familiar around the district.

Back in the 50s I can remember there being a couple of drapers, a shoe shop, a stationer, several dairies, a bakery, at least two grocers, three garages and the movies were on in the weekends . . . Well most of that has gone from Riverton but all the pubs in the district have survived! What does that tell you about our priorities?

There is something very special about our country pubs . . . A very special culture that doesn't present any feeling of unease that is often felt in a city pub. Let's stay loyal to these very special places of congregation so that they stay a part of our wonderful rural lifestyle.

Contemplation

I've often wondered what whitebait fishers talk about or contemplate whilst waiting for "a run" of the small white fish on their favourite river. These two fellows were leaning on the rail of their jetty the day I made this drawing — they are not imaginary — the bloke on the left was wearing a blue sweater! They'll know who they are and will most certainly recognise their hut... This is a typical "camp", one of many on the Aparima on the western side of the bridge. Until the recent spell of breezy weather the fish were running pretty well so I'm told and I was the recipient of a very generous meal of "bait" courtesy of my old friend Audrey McElvey... To get back to the riverside conversations I imagine are conducted by the Ladies and Gentlemen of the Aparima — I suppose politics are high on the agenda followed by local gossip, family and the cost of living... no doubt some of the retired folk will be speculating as to when they will get their hip replacement or prostrate operation and I'm sure the names of Winston, Jenny, Bill and Jim will be tossed around along with the date of the next election. The Aparima River played a large part in the early Maori history of this province. Ngatimamoe made their final stand in Southland after Ngai Tahu had conquered Rakiura (Stewart Island). Some historians say that the Ngai Tahu chief Kaweriri drove Ngatimamoe up the Aparima River, overwhelming them, causing them to withdraw as far away as Te Anau... So the quiet Aparima has certainly known some turbulent times.

Flecks' Farm Garage

John Stuart, a near neighbour of mine, can often be seen around this old garage, cutting and stacking timber from the trees he's tidied up on the property. A few years ago I did a series of drawings of the many buildings on the Fleck farm — one of which I used as a cover picture on my last published sketchbook. The homestead, probably built at the turn of the century, was a showpiece, with beautiful gardens and established trees. Parts of this property's former glory can still be traced, with a trellis archway still standing all on its own . . . Apparently John-Willie Fleck built this home for his new Irish bride in the days when the garage would have housed either a horse-drawn carriage or an early model motor car. According to the history of the Methodist church in Riverton, the Rev. Prosser thanked those who had contributed (in 1932) towards the final payments on the parsonage, thus rendering the church property unencumbered. James Fleck donated forty one pounds and five shillings ($82.50) towards the parson's motor car, two hundred and two pounds and sixpence ($404.05) towards the Sunday School and a quantity of furniture. George Fleck donated five pounds ($10.00) towards the same appeal. I presume the James Fleck mentioned above is a member of the well known local family, who still farm in the district.

Riverton War Memorial

After I had drawn this war memorial I climbed back up the hill to read closely what had been inscribed on this very commanding structure . . . Above the marble slabs that record the names of the locals who gave their lives in the Great War of 1914-18 are inscribed the messages "Grant them O Lord eternal rest" — "Their Name Liveth forever more" — "To the Glory of God and in memory of those of this town and district who gave their lives in the Great War 1914-18" and when those names are added up they tell us that 81 young men were cut down in their prime and 21 years later another 20 young men gave their lives during the 1939-45 conflict. We all agree that in hindsight it was a senseless waste of humanity, but at the same time, when I was growing up, it was an "Heroic struggle of Good" versus evil and we were carried along with it. . . . In 1961 Mr W. D. Morrison of the local R.S.A met with the local Council to arrange the financing of new marble slabs and the accompanying inscriptions. In March 1961 J. Fraser and Son tendered successfully for the removal of names — the erection of two new marble slabs and the re-lettering and replacement of two existing slabs for the princely sum of seventy eight pounds twelve shillings and sixpence! By the look of the present state of the memorial it needs someone to administer some more loving care and soon I hope.

The Nurses' Home

Apparently the earliest records of the Wallace and Fiord hospital in Riverton don't tell us much about the date of the inception of Health services in the town. A Dr. G. W. Grabham was the inspector of Hospitals for the colony in 1883 and he wrote a report on what was going on at that time . . . "It is a wooden building situated on high ground a little way from the town. There's a ward for each sex. Kitchen, wash-house, dispensary and three small rooms for steward and matron".

The Nurses' home was completed in May of 1932 and dedicated by the laying of a stone — which stated "This stone was laid by James C. Johnston Chairman of Wallace and Fiord Hospital Board on the 19th May 1932. Geo. O. Cassels Secretary. Stacey Walker Builder." There were two attics in the main building, one of which was occupied by a servant, but no mention of where the nursing staff slept. However, that was in 1883 and by the time this fine building was finished the nurses were undoubtedly being looked after in a far more humane way.

Jeremy's Bivouac

On the 15th of February 1997 I left Riverton for one of the more momentous events of my life. On Tuesday 18th I broadcast live to Foveaux Radio from the Solander Islands at about 8.45 a.m. This is what I had to report . . .

"Today is the beginning of Day Three of one of the most challenging adventures I've ever participated in. After 36 hours in the good ship "Howard James" (skippered by Ron Bull and crewed by son Rewi) we landed on what is laughingly referred to as a beach, getting drenched as a result! You see, there are no sandy stretches to loll upon, just huge rocks, some the size of the radio studio we broadcast in each day . . . and another thing for you to ponder is that our very small two man tent occupies the only really flat piece of ground on this huge 100 hectare rock — the result of volcanic eruption and a coalition government. All around it is a strip of rocks — then it rears a thousand feet or more, almost vertically!

Walking around — let alone filming and drawing it — is indeed a feat of endurance. We share our little piece of the island with many seals (there are about 5,000 of them on the island). Our neighbours are but metres away from me at this moment and they stink like you would not believe! But despite the weather we have shot some great footage for what I think will be a great film. Apart from myself there's Kim Westerkof, Geographic Wildlife Photographer; Jeremy Carrol from the Department of Conservation; and Cameraman Dave Asher." This drawing, made from our tent above, is of Jeremy's Bivouac — a simple fly strung up above an almost flat area strewn with rocks . . . Somehow or other Jeremy managed to sleep in this shelter, but when I come to recollect the adventure, we were so tired at the end of the day that we could have slept on a clothesline.

The Howard James

I made this drawing shortly after it had arrived back from taking a party of us down to "The Rock" — otherwise known as the Solander Islands which guard the western approach to Foveaux Strait.

In March 1770, Lieutenant James Cook and the crew got their first view of this remarkably high island which rises 1100 ft straight up out of the ocean . . . but our trip in the Howard James is another story which I will share with you at a later date. I asked the skipper of this steel hulled boat (Ron Bull) how it got its name and he told me he thought it was named after one of the engineers responsible for its construction. It's 27 years old and still as seaworthy and sturdy as it was on launching day. Ron first went to sea with his parents as a small boy on their annual pilgrimage to the Muttonbird Island. His career as a fisherman began at age 17 with well known fishing identity Doug Bradshaw in the days when communication with shore was primitive, staying away for up to six weeks at a time . . . "Our families must have done a lot of worrying then" he mused. "That's 40 years ago now!"

For the past five years son Rewi has been his crew . . . they fish around the rock for their crayfish quota and go codding and trawling from Preservation to Jacksons Bay. Ron's father, grandfather and uncles have all been fishermen in our part of New Zealand and as I sat with him in the wheelhouse of the Howard James the other day and observed the ready smile and twinkling eyes, I thought to myself "There's a lot of fishing in you yet, Ron" . . . He left me with this thought: "The sea can be a good friend but a bad master" . . . wise words from a wily mariner.

The Pub at Fairfax

In 1891 the Fairfax Blacksmith was Mr W. Reidie, the Manager of the Dairy Factory was J. McKinnon, and Jim Sutherland was both Post Master and Storekeeper, but perhaps the glue that held this tiny village together was the Shamrock Hotel run by the Proprietress Mrs C. Callaghan. It's not surprising that this was the only establishment that survived well into the present century and though it seems to be falling into a state of disrepair these days it still looks like a typical country pub. The advertisement in the directory of the day told us that Mrs Callaghan offered "Good accommodation, good Liquors and a Billiard table" . . .

The first time I ever set foot in the Hotel was in the early 60s. I was attending a party at the home of Rodger Jackman, who farmed down the road, when someone suggested we pop on down to the "Shamrock" and pick up a piano player by the name of Gill Dech. His recording of "Robin's Return" was one of the biggest sellers ever in this country and there was quite a bit of excitement among the guests who had never met him personally, including myself.

The legendary Frank Stapp had told me about Gill's fondness for the demon drink and how he often hid away on a big binge at the Shamrock Hotel at Fairfax. On one occasion he apparently stepped out onto the verandah that faced the road, quite a bit the worse for wear and toppled over onto the walkway below . . . He was obviously well enough lubricated to be in a totally relaxed state and didn't do very much damage to his frame. He lived to play another day!

Our party progressed well as Gill was in fine form with more than enough fuel aboard to enable him to play through most of the night. Wonderful memories of a great pub and a legendary musician.

Our host Rodger Jackman played rugby for Otautau and captained the team in 1960 and if I remember rightly he had a run for Southland about the same time.

The Last Mail Box

Around Southland and Otago in the late 1800s there was a Post Office in almost every small town and village — the Post Office was the centre of the Universe — Hirstfeld, Colac Bay, Riverton, Otautau, Wyndham, Orepuki — little towns that had a Post office until the time of great change and "Rodger Douglas" . . . can you remember just what you could do at the Post Office? My memory goes back to the time when you could buy a Post Office Money Order — send a telegram — make a toll call in one of those amazingly soundproof, green baize-lined phone boxes — register your car — pay in or withdraw money from the savings bank — pay your radio licence and you could, if need be, get married in the Postmaster's Office . . . Yes, Postmasters were as valid as your local Justice of the Peace. But what intrigued me was the Post Office architecture and fittings. Beautiful polished wood fixtures — brass handles and rails . . . the counter and the cubicles were wonderful examples of the woodworker's art and the native heart timber used just got better the more it was leaned upon — rubbed against and handled by the thousands of customers the Post Office serviced. No materials were spared in the building of these fine structures, and good examples were phone boxes and letter boxes — the English cast iron post box with his or her Royal Cypher are now treasured artifacts — these were followed by very stout wooden rectangular structures — painted bright red and they seemed to be everywhere. When all the reorganisation was going on I travelled around Otago and Southland recording the buildings, the phone boxes, Post boxes and all the other paraphernalia that went to make up the old Post and Telegraph Department. It was indeed a huge part of our Country heritage. This was the last letter box left in Riverton on the corner of Downing and Bath Streets and it had a great view of my favourite estuary. Shortly after I drew it this little bit of history disappeared.

The Pioneer Cottage

It's nearly thirty years since I did this drawing of a wooden colonial style cottage which still stands on the high ground above what was the Railway Station and timber yard at Longwood . . . also in this settlement was a working dairy factory — "Hekeia", one of the many throughout Southland. Well known identity Roly More left Invercargill as a young fellow to work in the Longwood timber yard. At that time there were three mills supplying the yard from the Pourakino Valley and all the timber was hauled out by More's Tram. This cottage has, since I drew it, been restored and changed somewhat to serve as a holiday home with a great view of the Pourakino landscape. Originally this cottage would have had a narrow passageway running from the front, dividing two tiny rooms. At the back were the kitchen and bathroom and usually a wash house in a lean to. I can remember visiting houses like this during my childhood and wondering how a couple and up to four or five kids could possibly live in such conditions. But somehow many families did and I suppose it was because of the love and support they gave each other that they survived and raised good young people.

John Husband

Pahia Dairy Company

You pass through Pahia on your way to that Scenic delight "Cosy Nook". On your left are the remains of the Dairy Factory complete with a fine brick smoke stack. When I first drew this relic about 20 years ago the water tank still stood proud, a testimony to the art of the cooper — a long lost art. I spent many of my school holidays in the Hawkes Bay village of Norsewood with my Grandfather and an uncle who were respectively manager and first assistant of the local Butter Factory and since these days my fascination for the architecture and culture of Dairy Factories hasn't waived. They all had a similar style and feel about them and as I've pottered around the few remaining factories still standing I find it easy to relive my childhood . . . The landing stages where the trucks and drays pulled in to unload the cargo of milk or cream — the boiler rooms where the energy was generated with the help of coal — the churn rooms and sometimes the remains of the long vats where fine New Zealand Cheddar had its beginnings. When I came to Southland there seemed to be a factory on every country corner. Now there is one, but let's hope that the trend of boutique cheese factories continues to move south. With a vineyard in Waikaia and a few cheese makers scattered throughout Southland we will be a province of taste as well as productivity.

Te Tua School

I wonder if there is anyone alive today who actually went to school in this tiny place of learning . . . in about 1885 one Hugh Erskine arrived at Papatotara and settled on the west bank of the Waiau. He cleared himself some bush and built a home, but not far behind him was a horde of sawmillers who worked their way west from Orepuki, through Waihoaka, Te Wae Wae, Te Tua and on to Tuatapere. Before our rural population became as mobile as they are today there were many tiny schools scattered throughout provinces like Southland. Wild Bush School is one such that has been left alone, probably because it's also a memorial to the fallen locals in two World Wars. My first school wasn't much bigger than this one . . . built of wood with the very familiar astricled windows which we gazed out of endlessly while searching for an answer to the interminable questions that were posed. In one corner of the classroom stood a coke burning stove — that was the entire heating system, so if you were very lucky enough to have a desk close to the warmth you got through a cold winter pretty comfortably. But don't let's forget "The Monitors" — the Coke Monitor, the Milk Monitor, the Blackboard Monitor and the Flag Monitor! Yes we ran up the flag every morning before class and saluted it. Silly sentimentalists? Or proud of our country — take your pick.

Riverton Post Office

From the files of the Western Star of Friday 18th of August 1911 came the news, in the local and general column, that "Riverton's new post office was completed on Tuesday of that week — but there was still a problem! The plaster was still wet, meaning that occupation was still some weeks away. The outside appearance is similar to the recently erected office in Wyndham. The residential part of this fine building compromises four rooms, kitchen, bathroom and pantry. The contractor for the work was Mr Lyder who carried out the work in the most satisfactory way" . . . At the time of the opening of this new addition to the business district of Riverton the postmaster was a Mr McKinnon . . . In 1883 the postmaster telegraphist was a Mr F. Teesdale and in 1891 this same position was held by Mr W. McHutchison and the collector of H.M. customs was H. McHutchison, no doubt of the same family. On the 26th of September the business of the postal department was finally shifted to the new building and the doors swung open for the first time to the public the day after. No formal opening was held on this day — this was carried out at a later date. Thankfully we still have this fine building in the form of "Prints and Presents" thanks to the efforts of the late Graham Watson.

The Hospital Cottage

This cottage stands just inside the rear entrance of what was originally known as the Wallace and Fiord Hospital. Prior to 1889 the old barracks building was the hospital and up to 1879 Dr. Monkton was the Medical Officer but he only attended when required. In 1889 a new up-to-date hospital was built with two wards to accommodate 30 patients and the cost was £2,000 ($4,000). No one I have spoken to knows when the little cottage was built and what it was used for . . . I would hazard a guess that it was built for a caretaker or night-watchman or even the person who attended the boiler house.

The small structure sticking out from the wall next to the chimney is what I remember as a meat safe.

The air passed through it to keep the meat, milk and butter cool, access of course was from inside and this was pre-refrigerator days . . . another intriguing feature was the chimney made of galvanised flat iron.

No doubt someone out there knows what this little gem was used for over the years, so let us know.

A Villa with a View

The Bay Villa began to appear around 1905. This fine example is at 16 Dallas Street here in Riverton. It has light panes above the double hung windows, fretwork, brackets, tall chimneys and a panel effect in the gable . . . The return verandah and double gables sit on a sturdy concrete base which elevates this stately wooden home, giving it a wonderful view of the harbour and Jacobs River. It's to be hoped it is kept in good order so that in the early part of the year 2000 it can claim to be another "Riverton Stately" that's reached its hundredth year. And not far away is the year 2037 when our town will be 200 years old.

74

Three Cottages

These three cottages on Palmerston Street really sum up Riverton and its beginnings . . . Across the road is an equally important slice of local history in the Daniels' home, which is in the process of being restored back to its former glory. These neatly kept homes are fine examples of early colonial architecture which began in the 1840s. Early records tell us that in the years from 1878 to 1892 these dwellings were occupied by the Edwards, Flowers and Hancock families. Not only were they a roof over the heads of these folk but at least one of them served as the business premises of one James Hancock who was the village Bootmaker around 1891. Richard Simonka is in the process of restoring the cottage on the left of the drawing. This cottage has a double gable with steeper pitch than the others, which accounts for the attic windows which can be seen on the west side . . . We must be grateful to those people who have almost a lifetime of maintenance ahead of them to allow us to enjoy these tangible reminders of Riverton's past.

"The Enterprise"

As I drive home each afternoon I catch a glimpse of the aft end of "the Enterprise" moored just near the south end of the bridge . . . it's always appealed to me as a very balanced "lady of the sea" particularly viewed from the rear! Gone are any pretensions of political correctness practised by me, but I think hot blooded men will always turn and admire a shapely woman walking away from them . . . This boat was built (one of four) in 1945 by Miller and Tunnage at Port Chalmers. Constructed of Kauri it is, according to its owner of six years, Peter Young, a great sea boat. It was previously owned by Peter Leask for 20 years. The only major alteration in its 54 year history is a change to the wheelhouse — shifted from aft to midships. Two crew man this fine little boat in our sometimes tempestuous waters of the south . . . long may these small fishing operations prosper — this is what fishing is all about.

A Cottage by the Sea

When I first arrived in Southland in the early 50s I discovered Orepuki and this tiny cottage crouched in the lee of a bank and some trees which almost embraced it. Directly behind it is a steep bank leading to one of the most spectacular beaches I've seen anywhere including a few overseas! There was someone living in this picturesque dwelling when I first ventured off the road to check out the story I'd heard about a tunnel which led from the rear of the house down to the beach. I've forgotten who greeted me on that day nearly 40 years ago but I do remember that I didn't get an answer to my question about the tunnel. Real smugglers' cove stuff that I never ever confirmed. Perhaps some reader will fill me in with the details. Two names associated with the cottage are Turnbull and Hogget both residents during its long life which I believe began in the last century.

Triple Towers

George Valentine Prinz came to Preservation Inlet as a ten year old to work as a Coopers assistant, all the way from Sydney, where he was born on St. Valentine's Day 1827. Just imagine how daunting that it would be for a ten year old in this day and age! He worked for Captain Howell — spent a year on Codfish Island, then back to work for George Stirling at Bluff — he then gave goldmining in Australia a try, did a number of other things but the lure of the land finally got the better of him. He purchased a large parcel of land at Sandy Point then a 7,000 acre property at Pahia — he settled four of his sons on farms in this area and three of their homes were easily distinguished by their turrets. George Jnr's home had one turret and that home was on the Mt. Victoria property. William's home at Pahia had two turrets and John, otherwise known as Barney, had three turrets on his property at Monkey Island — poor old Harry who farmed at Ruahine was towerless! This fine old villa and its near relation still stand proudly in our district. Long may they remain.

Flecks' Farm

I wandered one day — many years ago — up a long driveway to this house, fully expecting it to be inhabited . . . you see, you couldn't really tell from the road but I had always assumed as I drove past that behind many trees and shrubs, there lived a family. I wasn't too disappointed when I found that it was deserted, because I enjoyed just sitting, imagining what it had been like in its heyday. By the look of the design it was probably built at the turn of the century and I subsequently found out that the property has been in the same Fleck Family for more than a hundred years!

As well, this family has a hall named after them. The tiny structure in the foreground is, no doubt, a place of many memories and great and profound decisions would have been reached inside those three walls and a door . . . But — don't go looking for it, it's gone! A lush pasture is in its place . . .